101 Questions About
COPYRIGHT
LAW

Andrew Alpern

Special Counsel to Hughes Hubbard & Reed LLP

DOVER PUBLICATIONS, INC.
Mineola, New York

Bibliographical Note

101 Questions About Copyright Law is a new work, first published by Dover Publications, Inc., in 1999.

Library of Congress Cataloging-in-Publication Data

Alpern, Andrew.
    101 questions about copyright law / Andrew Alpern.
        p.   cm.
    ISBN 0-486-40448-X (pbk.)
    1. Copyright—United States—Miscellanea.   I. Title.
KF2995.A528   1999
346.7304'82—dc21   98-41538
                                                         CIP

Manufactured in the United States of America
Dover Publications, Inc., 31 East 2nd Street, Mineola, N.Y. 11501

A WARNING AND A DISCLAIMER

Change is inherent to the United States's system of law, and this is particularly true at the dynamic intersection of the increasingly pervasive digital technology and the established principles of copyright protections. The answers to the questions posed in this book take into account recent changes to the statutes governing copyright, but the interpretations of those measures as set forth in judicial decisions only will emerge over time. Adding to the uncertainty, built into the new laws are requirements for periodic reevaluation of certain provisions by the Copyright Office and by Congress. Some elements of these laws may evolve, and others may prove unworkable and be repealed. The only assurance we can give concerning the continued reliability of our answers is that there are no iron-clad assurances to be given.

The most dramatic changes in the law involve digital technology and the Internet. Digital transmissions of copyrighted material, encryption of information, and commercial transactions in cyberspace all now fall within the ambit of the copyright law. While this little book touches lightly upon these subjects, its answers only can alert the reader to the need for further research and investigation in this rapidly evolving area of intellectual property law.

This book offers a selective description of some aspects of U.S. copyright law and provides general advice and guidance. The information furnished does not necessarily apply to any given situation. It should not be used as a replacement for specific counsel from an attorney or other suitably qualified professional who understands all the applicable law and who is familiar with all the relevant facts and circumstances.

Introduction

What we now know as copyright law is used primarily as a means of protection to *benefit* authors and other creators, but when it originated in England copyright law was intended as protection *against* authors. The introduction of the printing press into England in 1476 spawned a large publishing industry that distributed many books the Crown considered seditious, heretical, or otherwise undesirable. To control books written by authors who wrote things the Crown didn't want distributed, a decree was issued in 1534 that no book could be published without a license. In 1556 a publishing monopoly was granted to the Stationers' Company (a guild of established publishers loyal to the Crown) by making those licenses available only from them. The licensing laws were problematical, and they were allowed to expire in 1695. With authors now free to publish without having to grant exclusive and perpetual rights to the Stationers' Company, independent publishers not controlled by the ancient Stationers' guild proliferated. These independents rapidly took business away from the older publishing houses. The Stationers protested loudly in Parliament.

The result was the innovative Statute of Anne of 1710. Although it gave the Stationers partial and temporary relief from their new competition, the Statute was more significant because, under its provisions, authors were granted certain protections for their works. Giving as its ultimate goal the enhancement of the public welfare through the dissemination of knowledge, the Statute stated that its purpose was "the encouragement of learned men to compose and write useful work." On this foundation our modern copyright law was constructed.

When the first United States copyright law was signed into law by President George Washington in 1790, the arts and sciences were cultivated through slow access to prior knowledge available only to those in physical proximity to that knowledge, which was contained in expensive and often minimally distributed books. For two centuries, the system functioned at a level deemed acceptable by many people, though it denied full access to those arts and sciences to vast portions of the world's populations. Now, within one-twentieth of that timespan, there has developed a promise, rapidly being fulfilled, of access to all the world's libraries and knowledge through tiny strands of copper or fiber optics, delivered *anywhere* where a telephone connection can be made.

1. **What is the basic concept underlying the system of copyright protection in the United States and where does it come from?**

The Constitution of the United States, written in 1787, says that the Congress shall have the power "To promote the Progress of Science and useful Arts, by securing for limited Times to Authors and Inventors the exclusive Right to their respective Writings and Discoveries." Underlying this simple statement was the recognition that the new nation needed to encourage the accumulation of intellectual capital among its citizens, and the belief that the most effective way to do this was to offer an economic incentive for the creation of what we call *intellectual property*.

2. **What is intellectual property?**

Intellectual property is a term for certain *results* of ideas, but not the ideas themselves. There are various forms of intellectual property. These forms are categorized by the legal frameworks that have been developed to encourage the creation of intellectual property by converting *ideas* into *results*.

A **utility patent** recognizes the creation of several types of intellectual property: a new and useful machine, process, article of manufacture, or composition of matter, or any new and useful improvement on any of those things. Under the federal patent law, a utility patent grants a twenty-year right, beginning on the date the patent application was filed, to exclude others from making, using, or selling the patented item.

A **design patent** recognizes the creation of a new, original, and *ornamental* design for an article of manufacture. The design must exist physically as part of a functional manufactured item yet be itself nonfunctional and conceptually separate from the item's function. A design patent lasts for fourteen years from the date the patent is granted.

A **plant patent** recognizes the invention or discovery and the asexual reproduction of any distinct and new variety of plant, excluding a tuber-propagated plant or one found in an uncultivated state. A plant patent is valid for seventeen years from the date the patent is granted.

A **trademark or a service mark** is a distinctive word, phrase, symbol, or other recognizable device that identifies a product or a service and distinguishes it from other, similar products or services in the marketplace for those products or services. This sort of protection for intellectual property is available in several forms, under both federal and various state laws, and thus can differ from place to place.

A **trade secret** is any information (such as a formula, method, or source of supply), or compilation of information (such as a client list) that: is used or useful in a business, is kept secret, and gives a competitive advantage over those who do not know or use it. The law of trade secrets is the only mechanism for protecting *ideas,* apart from contractual confidentiality agreements. It is state law, varying by jurisdiction and found in both statutes and the common law.

A **copyright** protects the *expression* of an idea as fixed in some tangible medium. Protecting only the expression and not the idea is reasonable. After all, what person could present sufficient proof of having been the first to have a particular idea? On the other hand, the first person to register a copyright on the expression of an idea can readily be identified. The goals of copyright law include providing incentives to authors to create new ways of manifesting ideas, so copyright protection is given only when the expression is original and was produced by the exertion of at least some *minimal* level of intellectual creativity. For example, merely arranging a list of names into alphabetical order would not involve enough creativity to merit protection, but *selecting and categorizing* those names by country of origin might.

The **right of publicity** is a form of intellectual property right that protects the name, image, and identifying persona of a natural person (but not that of a corporation or other entity) against unwanted or unauthorized use. Infringement of this right is a form of unfair competition and is actionable in a lawsuit as a commercially wrongful activity. The right of publicity differs from the right of personal privacy in that its infringement results in commercial disadvantage or economic loss, while an infringement of the right of personal privacy results in emotional distress or social detriment.

3. What sorts of expressions of ideas fit within the framework of U. S. copyright protections?

The concept of copyright began with words—a few sentences, a book, a poem, a set of song lyrics, a narrative description, a set of instructions for doing something—but the concept has been expanded over the years to accommodate many newer forms of intellectual expression that humans have devised. Copyright protection may exist for a painting, a still photograph or an entire movie, a sculpture, the choreography of a dance when expressed in dance notation or filmed, a piece of music when transcribed in musical notation or recorded, a computer software program, a game, a chart, an architectural construction drawing, even an architectural design as expressed in the finished building. The list of copyrightable works covers only eight categories: a) literary works, b) musical works, c) dramatic works, d) pantomimes and choreographic works, e) pictorial, graphics, and sculptural works, f) motion pictures and other audiovisual works, g) sound recordings, and h) architectural works. Although these classifications may appear to be narrowly restrictive, they actually are interpreted very broadly, and a new creation that has never before been seen or described may be copyrightable if it can reasonably fit within one of the listed categories. Thus, a computer program can be registered as a "literary work."

4.   How can internal computer-speak be considered to be literature?

The copyrightable category is *literary work*, not *literature*. One of the wonders of legal statutes is that they can define words in ways that people who are not lawyers find baffling—and two different statutes can define the same word in two different ways, with later court decisions determining what those definitions mean in particular cases. A literary work, as defined in the copyright statute, is a work, other than an audiovisual work, "expressed in words, numbers, or other verbal or numerical symbols or indicia, regardless of the nature of the material objects, such as books, periodicals, manuscripts, phonorecords, film, tapes, disks, or cards, in which they are embedded."

As originally enacted, the 1976 copyright law retained the preexisting "rule of doubt" on computer programs, under which the Copyright Office accepted for registration any computer programs that were in humanly readable form, but left for the courts the question of whether such programs merited copyright protection at all. Congress had passed the 1976 Copyright Act with the understanding that copyright applicability to computer programs needed more study. It appointed the National Commission of New Technological Uses of Copyrighted Works ("CONTU") to study the matter. In 1980, the CONTU report's recommendations were adopted as an amendment to the copyright law. The law now defines a computer program as "a set of statements or instructions to be used directly or indirectly in a computer in order to bring about a certain result," and sets forth certain limitations on the exclusive rights that the owner of a copyright in a computer program holds. Because of the words "directly or indirectly" in the definition of a computer program, copyright protection extends to a program as originally written in human-readable form in BASIC, C, or other "high-level language," and also as written in the series of ones and zeros understandable by the computer itself, which is typically a machine translation of the high-level program. The first step produces "source code" and the second step yields "object code" or "binary executable code." All of these forms are copyrightable literary works.

5. Are there creative works that are not eligible for copyright protection?

While human creativity is seemingly boundless, not all of it becomes automatically entitled to copyright protection upon creation. This includes intellectual accomplishments that reasonably would seem to fall within the scope of the eight categories listed above. One of the requirements for copyrightability is that the work be fixed in a tangible form of expression; it is not enough that the work can be perceived. Thus, the choreography of a dance that is improvised and has not been recorded in dance notation or on film or video is not protected by copyright, nor is an extemporaneous speech that has not been written down or recorded. However, such expressions of ideas may be covered by a noncopyright form of protection, such as a confidentiality and nondisclosure agreement signed by those who see the dance or hear the speech.

Copyright protection is not available for the title of a book or other creative work even if the work itself is copyrightable, nor for the name of a chemical compound, a play, or a software program. It is not available for a catchy short phrase that might be perfect for advertising a new product, nor for a familiar symbol, a minor variation in an existing design, or a recipe that merely lists the ingredients of the dish—even if those ingredients never before were brought together. Copyright law does not extend to an idea, a procedure, a method, a system, a process, a concept, a principle, a discovery, or a device . . . all as distinguished from descriptions, explanations, or illustrations of those things.

The *design* of an ornamental piece of sculpture can be copyrighted, as can the *drawing* of the design of a useful article, but there is no copyright protection for the *design* of a useful article (such as an article of clothing or a household appliance). To the extent that the *design* of that article can exist independent of the useful article, however, it may be within the copyright sphere. Thus, the design of an elegant and unusual belt buckle was given design protection when it was shown that it was being worn as a decorative embellishment as much as for its more prosaic function as a device to secure a belt.

6. Is eligibility for copyright protection governed by international copyright law?

There is no such thing as an "international copyright" to protect copyrightable material throughout the world. Protection from unauthorized use in any given country depends on the national law of that country. This concept of territoriality generally limits the reach of a country's laws to the borders of that country. However, countries can sign treaties and conventions that have the effect of law in those countries once they have been ratified. The United States, along with most other countries, offers protections to foreign works in conformance with the two primary international copyright conventions, the Berne Convention and the Universal Copyright Convention.

7. What is the Berne Convention?

The Berne Union for the Protection of Literary and Artistic Property (the "Berne Convention") is a multinational treaty created in 1886 that sets forth several basic copyright principles to which each signatory country must adhere in its national copyright laws, as follows: a) *Nationality.* Each country must offer at least the same level of copyright protection to works originating in another Berne Convention country as the first country offers to works of its own citizens. b) *Formalities.* Copyright protection must be automatic and must not depend on registration of the copyright or inclusion of a copyright notice or symbol. c) *Duration.* Copyright must be effective for a minimum term of the author's life plus fifty years. d) *Moral rights.* Certain defined rights of attribution and integrity must be protected under the signatory's national law. e) *Independence.* Copyright protection must be independent of the existence of protection in the country of origin. f) *Exclusive rights.* The copyright holder must have exclusive rights of reproduction, translation, adaptation, and public performance of the copyrighted work. In 1989, the United States joined the Berne

Convention by becoming a signatory and by amending the United States copyright law in a way that meets the Berne strictures but ensures that only the United States copyright law governs copyright litigation in the United States, and not the provisions of the Berne Convention itself. As of this writing, 119 of the world's 192 countries had joined the Berne Convention.

8. What is the Universal Copyright Convention?

The Universal Copyright Convention (the "UCC") was created in 1952 under the auspices of UNESCO as a less restrictive alternative to the Berne Convention. Its provisions were structured to accommodate the then-current United States copyright law of 1909, with the expectation that the United States would become a party to it. The United States did so in 1955, joining a group of nations that includes some that are not signatories to the Berne Convention. With the United States now a member of the Berne Convention, the UCC has lost much of its importance, but it retains significance concerning those countries that are members solely of the UCC.

9. Does the U.S. membership in these two international conventions mean that the requirements of the U.S. Copyright Law are all that need to be met?

Although U.S. law now meets all copyright protection requirements of the Berne Convention, problems of lack of copyright protection may arise in countries that are members of the UCC but not of the Berne Convention. However, even if a work cannot find protection under the UCC or the Berne Convention, in some instances protection may be available by means of bilateral agreements between the United States and certain other countries, or under specific provisions of a country's national laws. If it is important that a work have copyright protection in a specific country or countries, the relevant laws should be investigated prior to publication anywhere, since the protection that is available may depend on the timing and method of publication. As some countries offer little or no copyright protection to foreign authors, this should be considered in deciding upon the scope of international distribution for specific works. Careful research and advance planning is important for any work with an international market.

10. Which tangible media can be used to fix a copyrightable expression?

The number of eligible media is rapidly increasing. It includes any means by which expressions of ideas can be recorded. Paper is the most obvious, along with canvas for a painting, an emulsion for a photograph, cassette tape for both the words and the music to a song, a diskette for an interactive video game, a LAN network server or a hard drive for software or an electronic version of a report.

11. Once there is an original and at least minimally creative work fixed in a tangible medium of expression, what must be done to get it copyrighted?

The acts of creating the work and fixing it in a tangible medium of expression create the copyright under the federal Copyright Act of 1976, which superseded the Copyright Act of 1909 (with certain exceptions for preexisting works) and which replaced all state copyright laws. Registration is not required as a condition of copyright protection and the duration of that protection is not dependent on it. However, registration can bring with it definite advantages in the event that someone infringes upon the registered copyright. Copyright registration can be secured through the Copyright Office in Washington, D.C., by following procedures that are discussed later in this book.

12. In addition to registration of the copyright, isn't a copyright notice on the work required?

The requirements of copyright notice fall into three legal "eras." For works published prior to 1978, publication without a copyright notice in proper form and position meant forfeiture of the copyright to the public domain, with recapture only under very limited circumstances. For works first published after 1977 through April 1989, the copyright notice was still required but there were a few ways of making up for its omission, and the work didn't necessarily fall into the public domain if a proper notice was missing. Finally, effective May 1, 1989, the requirement for a copyright notice as a condition for copyright protection was eliminated from the United States Copyright Law as part of the changes necessary to enable the United States to become a member of the Berne Convention.

13. Does this lack of a notice requirement in the current version of the copyright law eliminate the need for a copyright notice?

A copyright notice should always be placed on the work if full copyright protection is desired. Although not required by the hundred-plus countries that are members of the Berne Convention, the copyright notice serves several important purposes. It is necessary for protection in the more than 70 countries that have not signed the Berne Convention; it precludes an infringer from claiming lack of knowledge of the copyright (and thus appearing to be an "innocent" infringer, who will get off lightly); and it generally serves as a deterrent to infringement by clearly proclaiming the existence, starting date, and ownership of the copyright.

14. What is the proper form for a copyright notice?

Its form is the c-in-a-circle or © symbol, or the word "Copyright," followed by the year the work was published, followed by the name of the owner of the copyright. When it is considered desirable to make it clear to users that the author takes the copyright protections especially seriously, a further statement such as "All rights of reproduction and distribution reserved" or a longer and more detailed prohibition against infringement can be useful. (A name and address to be used in requests for permission to reproduce the protected material can be added to such a statement.)

15. Is that the proper form for *all* copyright notices?

The required notice is slightly different for a phonorecord (which is any sort of format—record, tape, CD, laser disc, or methods not yet invented) for sound recordings (which are "works that result from the fixation of a series of musical, spoken, or other sounds, but not including the sounds accompanying a motion picture or other audiovisual work"). The form of the phonorecord notice is a p-in-a-circle or ℗ symbol, plus the year the work was first published as a sound recording, plus the name of the owner of the copyright in the sound recording.

16. Where should the copyright notice be placed?

The legal requirement is for it to be placed "in such manner and location as to give reasonable notice of the claim of copyright." This generally translates into a commonsense rule that can be flexible to suit the broad range of situations that copyright covers. Regardless of placement, the notice should be large enough to be easily read, and should be set apart from any surrounding text or graphic material. We are so used to seeing the notice in books in the position formerly mandated by the superseded copyright law of 1909 that the same position commonly has been used under the 1976 law as well. The notice should appear either on the title page, or on the verso of the title page (where the International Standard Book Number or ISBN, the Library of Congress cataloguing data, and various other small-print notices usually are placed). If the book is published in a loose-leaf or other format, with components that are readily separable, a small copyright notice at the bottom of each page or each component is needed. Notice placement for a magazine may be on the cover, or near the masthead or as part of it, or near the table of contents, or in some other location where logic suggests the reader would be expected to look if seeking the information in the notice. For a contribution to a magazine or other collective work, the copyright notice for each article or chapter can be placed near either the author's name or the title of the contribution, at the start of the item, or all of the notices can be placed together with the notice for the entire work. If the exclusive rights to each article are owned by the authors of the articles, placing each notice on the first page of the article to which it refers is best, because it most clearly presents the relevant information to the reader. Notices for individual illustrations should be placed in close proximity to those illustrations, unless all illustrations in the work are within the same copyright claim, in which case the notice can be placed next to the notice for the entire work. Where there are multiple claimants for various components or aspects of a work, putting all the copyright notices together is reasonable. Thus, for example, the reader can be informed that the total work is copyright 1999 by A, the translation is copyright 1998 by B, the illustrations are copyright 1997 by C, the chart on page 14 is copyright 1996 by D, and no copyright claim is made for government forms included as the appendix.

17.   Are there special rules for works other than books?

The same legal requirements and commonsense rules apply. The placement must "give reasonable notice" to the public of the copyright information. On a piece of sculpture, the copyright notice may be placed in any location where it is artistically appropriate, provided that it is readily visible to viewers. On a photograph or a painting, it should be placed on the front if artistically feasible, but it may be placed on the back, provided that the back readily can be seen under ordinary circumstances. For a software program or a CD-ROM, the notice should be placed on the disc label and on the first or title screen of the program, and also on the package and the instruction booklet, since these are separable items. For a movie, the notice should appear on the title screen, or with the credits, which may be at either the beginning or the end of the film. For a phonorecord, the notice should be included on the record, CD, or tape label, and on the sleeve, box, or other packaging. The copyright notice for an unpublished manuscript should be placed on the title page, primarily to deter infringers. The goal is to give the world notice of the copyright; the position of the notice must accomplish that aim.

18. Is the copyright notice sufficient or should an additional warning be used?

The copyright notice serves a legal purpose, but it also acts as a deterrent to infringers. Additional emphasis or further warnings may be advisable, particularly if it is likely that readers may have a strong interest in copying or otherwise using the material in the work. At the barest minimum, such additional notice would read "All Rights Reserved." A more emphatic version might say, "No part of this book may be reproduced in any form or by any means, whether mechanical or electronic, including any form of storage and retrieval system." When the copyright owner is willing to give permission for copying (with or without a royalty fee), instructions on where to write to obtain permission are useful. A stage play or screenplay needs a special warning to deter both professionals and amateurs from infringing upon the performance rights of the copyright owner, such as: "Professionals and amateurs are warned that this work is fully protected under the copyright law and may not be performed in public production, reading, adaptation, or reproduced in any way without permission first obtained from and a royalty paid to [XYZ Company, Address, Telephone and Fax Number, Web Site Address]."

19. Aren't there other notice symbols?

There are several, but they are used for other forms of intellectual property protection. A ^{TM} following a word or phrase indicates that a claim under state law is being made for that word or phrase as a trademark to describe a tangible object. If the symbol following the word is ^{SM}, the word or phrase is a service mark to describe some service that the claimant is offering. The r-in-a-circle or ® symbol means that the trademark or service mark word or phrase has been registered with the Patent and Trademark office in Washington, D.C., and is entitled to specific protections under the federal trademark law. Patented articles must be marked with the applicable patent number.

20. Who is the copyright owner whose name is part of the copyright notice?

Generally, the person who actually created the work is the owner of its copyright, and when there has been joint creation by several people, they are all equal joint owners, unless those joint creators have made an agreement for some other arrangement. A minor child may claim copyright, but state laws regulate the extent to which minors may make contracts. Thus, when a minor is the creator of the copyrightable work, legal counsel should be sought before attempting to register or enter into a contractual agreement concerning that work. An important exception to the basic copyright ownership scheme affects material created as work made for hire.

21. What is a work made for hire?

An employee who creates a work within the scope of his or her employment produces a "work made for hire." Copyright in that work is owned by that employee's employer. Contrary to near-universal intuitive belief, a work made for hire does *not* automatically result every time a work is commissioned for monetary remuneration. A specially commissioned work *can* be a work made for hire, but only if there is a written agreement specifically commissioning the work as a work made for hire, *and* the work falls within one of nine specific categories set forth in the copyright law. This curiously disparate list of potential works made for hire consists of: (1) a contribution to a collective work (an article for a magazine, for example); (2) a part of a motion picture or other audiovisual work; (3) a translation; (4) a supplementary work;

(5) a compilation; (6) an instructional text; (7) a test; (8) answer material for a test; (9) an atlas. Determining whether a specific work is a work made for hire can be a very difficult and complex legal task. In some critical cases it has resulted in long and expensive litigation.

22. Can ownership of a work made for hire be transferred?

The owner of the rights in a work made for hire, just as the owner of any copyright—whether it be the individual creator, the employer, or the commissioner of the work—can, even before registration of the copyright or before publication, transfer ownership to anyone by agreement, just as ownership of *any* property can be transferred.

23. What are those transferable rights of the copyright owner?

A copyright can be viewed as a bundle of exclusive (and individually transferable) rights, which include the right to make copies of the work, the right to distribute those copies to the public (by sale or otherwise), the right to create other works based on the work (derivative works), and the right to perform or display the work. Individual rights and subsidiary rights (often called "sub-rights") from that bundle can be rented or sold (this is the economic advantage that encourages the creation of the work). The owner can "license" to Publisher No. 1 the right to make softcover copies of the work in the United States, to Publisher No. 2 the softcover rights everywhere else in the world, to Publisher No. 3 the hardcover rights throughout the world, while retaining the right to market the work as a CD-ROM and as part of an electronic information service on the Internet. And all those licensed rights can be for limited time periods or for the entire term of the copyright. A license can be granted to someone who wants to translate the work into a foreign language, and another license can be granted to someone else who wants to turn the story into a television miniseries. The number of individual rights in the bundle that can be licensed out for a profit is limited only by the imagination of the copyright owner and the practical limitations of the marketplace.

24. Isn't there a new right for digital recordings?

Since the beginning of 1996, the copyright owner of a sound recording has had an exclusive digital transmission performance right, which is primarily applicable to on-line subscription services delivering music. This new right does not apply to broadcasts over the radio or on television, which are not transmitted digitally. Coupled with the new right is provision for a scheme of compulsory licensing and for the payment of royalties for the use of such licenses. Digital rights and limitations are complex. If you have a question about digital recordings or transmissions you may wish to research the matter.

25. How long does the copyright owner's bundle of rights remain exclusive?

For a work created after 1977 by an individual for his or her own account, the term of the copyright is for that person's lifetime plus seventy years (with the person's heirs enjoying the benefit of those additional years, unless—with some exceptions—the owner has already cashed in the rights for that period by selling them to someone else). If the work is a work made for hire, the copyright remains valid for 95 years from the date of publication, or 120 years from the date of its creation, whichever term is shorter. Transferring ownership of the copyright doesn't alter these periods. For a specific work created and first published before 1978, the period of its copyright protection depends on a number of factual questions, and the process of determining that period can be complex. Under the 1909 law, there was an initial 28-year term, measured from first publication, with a second 28-year term if the copyright was renewed in a timely and proper manner. In anticipation of the passage of the 1976 law, those copyrights that were in their renewal terms were extended, and, under a 1998 revision to the 1976 law, called the Sonny Bono Copyright Term Extension Act, those renewed copyrights were modified to last for 95 years from the date of original publication. For all other works first published prior to 1964, a 95-year term, measured from the date of first publication, was established, subject to timely renewal of the initial 28-year term being made. For works first published after 1963 and prior to 1978, the renewal requirement later was removed, but the 95-year copyright term based on the original date of first publication remained in place. Laying out all these rules against a chart of years yields the ultimate conclusion that copyright protection for all works first published at least 95 years ago has expired and—with only limited exceptions—those works all are now in the public domain.

However, because the 20-year extension of copyright duration enacted in 1998 will need to be interpreted by court cases, if the question
becomes of critical importance to you at any time, double-check the
then-current status of the law.

26. Are there special rules for works that have not been published?

For a post-1977 work, the copyright term is independent of publication, except in the case of the alternative methods for calculating its
duration that are noted above for a work made for hire. The provisions
of the copyright law determining duration of copyright are more complicated for a work created before 1978 but not published. If the author
of the work had been dead for at least 70 years on January 1, 1978, the
work would remain under copyright protection through the end of the
year 2002 and then would fall into the public domain, unless it had
been published by December 31, 2002. If it were published by that date,
the copyright protection would then be extended to the end of 2047.
(This is another stipulation of the law that is intended to encourage
publication.)

27. What happens to the copyright in unpublished works of authors who were alive on January 1, 1908?

If such an author had not been dead at least 70 years at the beginning of 1978, copyright in the unpublished work would endure until 70
years after his or her death, which could extend the copyright out to
the end of 2047 at the latest. If such a work is published before the end
of 2002, the copyright lasts until 70 years after the author's death, or
through the end of the year 2047, whichever is later (but see the warning at the front of this book).

28. Are the rules different for successive editions of a work?

No . . . *but.* The copyright term of a specific work cannot be
extended by publishing a new edition of it. However, a new edition is
likely to include changes to the original work, and perhaps additions to
it. Thus, the new edition is a "derivative work" that incorporates the
original work, with changes and additions. The copyright term of the
original work as embodied in the derivative work remains constant,

with the copyright term in the changes and additions being determined as a separate work. Generally, in such a case, at some point in time the copyright in the original work will expire and the original work will go into the public domain, but the changes added for the new edition will still be under copyright protection. As a practical matter, this means that the new edition as a whole remains protected, but anyone is free to produce a *different* revised edition of the original work.

29. What exactly is "publication"?

The date of publication, for purposes of the copyright law, is the date when copies of a copyrightable work are available to the public for sale, rental, loan, or other form of distribution. Here, the word public means persons who are not restricted from freely disclosing the contents of the work. It isn't necessary that anyone actually buy a copy or accept a free handout of one, as long as people *could* buy copies if they wanted to, or if copies were *offered* or otherwise made available for distribution. Offering to distribute copies for purposes of further distribution also constitutes publication, so that the date when a new book is available to a wholesaler is the date of publication for copyright purposes, even though the book may not actually be available to the ultimate reader for several weeks. When a phonorecord is available as described above, it constitutes the publication of the underlying work embodied in that phonorecord. Merely performing the work or playing the phonorecord, however, does not constitute publication, no matter how many people hear it. The year of publication is important, because it is a part of the copyright notice, and because it is the starting point for one of the measurements that determine the duration of certain forms of copyright protection.

30. What is excluded from the copyright owner's bundle of rights?

Even though a work in its entirety may be entitled to copyright protection, certain portions of it may be copied without violating that protection. Any *ideas* in the work (as opposed to the *expression* of those ideas), and any objective *facts* (which by definition are not creative), are not within the scope of the copyright. Any material in the work that is already in the *public domain* is also not within the scope of the copyright. A publication or other material issued by the federal government is, with very few exceptions, part of the public domain and may be freely used by everyone. Once a work's copyright expires, that work goes into the public domain and is available to all. As noted earlier, practically all works first published at least 95 years ago are in the public domain, as are works published before 1964 for which the initial 28-year copyright term under the 1909 law was not renewed. A work published before March 1, 1989, may have gone into the public domain by default if it was published without the then-mandated copyright notice.

31. Does the copyright owner have the right to prevent *all* copying of the work?

To foster the creation of new works, the copyright law permits a limited amount of mining of earlier material—even against the specific wishes of the owners of the copyrights in those preexisting works. This is called the *fair-use privilege*, and the *fair-use defense* may be used when a legal action is brought regarding a use that would otherwise be a copyright infringement.

32. What sort of "fair use" is protected against an infringement claim?

Whether a use falls within the privilege is not a simple yes-or-no matter. Fair use *may* exist where the purpose is for a critical review, to report news, for teaching, or for scholarship or research. The story does not end there, however. Before a determination can be made that the privilege applies, there must be a weighing of four factors: the purpose and character of the use; the nature of the copyrighted work; the amount and substantiality of the portion used, in relation to the copyrighted work as a whole; and the effect of the use on the market for the copyrighted work or its value. The United States Supreme Court called this the "equitable rule of reason" and said that it is necessary because it "permits courts to avoid rigid application of the copyright statute when, on occasion, it would stifle the very creativity which that law is designed to foster."

33. Does this mean that the Supreme Court has decided what is and is not fair use?

Unfortunately, no. It is clear that the subject is very complicated indeed. The Court has given some direction and guidance, though. In most situations that individuals might encounter, the issues can be simplified. One of the rights in the copyright bundle is the exclusive right to make copies of the work. Thus, on the surface, making a photocopy of even one page of a copyrighted book or magazine is an infringement. However, making photocopies of a few pages of such a work for one's personal use is considered fair use—copying a recipe from a magazine, or a maintenance technique from an auto manual, for example. Photocopying the entire book, even for personal use, would not be fair use, however, because it would obviate the need to purchase a copy of the book and thus would deprive the copyright owner of a rightful economic benefit.

34.   Is the copyright owner's economic benefit the key to whether "fair use" exists?

There are no "keys" or short answers when it comes to "fair use." However, economic benefit is the carrot the copyright law offers to writers and other creators to encourage their creativity and thereby to increase the country's intellectual capital. At the same time, preserving the copyright owner's economic stake in his or her work must be balanced against the good of the rest of society. Even a brief quotation from a book in a published review may in fact have a detrimental effect on the sales of that book if the author's writing is really terrible, yet using a quotation in a book review is still considered to be a fair use, because the public benefits from book reviews, and quotations help readers to evaluate the book under review. A parody or satire of an existing work, which by its nature usually has to include enough of the original work to enable readers to recognize what is being parodied, is generally considered to benefit society sufficiently to constitute fair use. Similarly beneficial to the public is the creation of new works of scholarship or research that quote or paraphrase earlier works and then build upon them, as are photocopies distributed as part of a not-for-profit educational program.

35.   Does the picture get any clearer if we ask what is *not* fair use?

Two important relevant factors are whether the copies are made for profit, and the nature of the purpose for which the copies are made. Photocopies made for a large internal training session by a profit-making corporation probably would not be protected by the fair-use privilege, even though the purpose of making the copies could be characterized as "teaching." The reason is that the ultimate goal is increasing the profits of the corporation: the teaching is merely a means to that end. In a parallel situation, a well-known chain of copy shops was making large profits from assembling custom "textbooks" for college professors by copying large quantities of copyrighted material selected by the professors, binding the sheets, and selling the resulting books to the students of those professors. The professors were not profiting from the sale of the custom-made books, which they used in teaching, but the copy shop's use of the copyrighted material was entirely for profit, and to the detriment of the copyright owners, so the court said the practice was not fair use and must cease.

36. Isn't there *some* simple guideline to follow?

A relatively simple rule says that extensive use of copyrighted material in a book published commercially for profit, or even a brief quotation from a copyrighted work, when used in a commercial magazine advertisement, will not be considered fair use. There are anomalies even with this simple rule, though. Even in a commercial setting, fair use has been found when the use was socially beneficial, when the economic effect on the copyright owner was minimal, and when proper attribution was given. If you are determined to use someone else's material, the safest approach is to use a short quotation that is a small portion of the copyrighted work and that does not form the heart of the quoted work, and to give a complete and correct attribution. For any reuse of copyrighted material that will be used by the general public, or by any large number of people, it is best to obtain written permission to use the excerpted material, thereby mooting the entire question. In a commercial or business setting, such as within a corporation or a professional practice, valid fair-use copying seldom occurs. Large-scale or systematic copying in a business or commercial setting, or reproducing copyrighted works in business publications, *requires* that permission of the copyright owner be obtained. Remember, if the use of a work without permission serves as a replacement or substitute for the original work, thereby depriving the copyright owner of one of the economic benefits of the copyright, it is unlikely that the fair-use defense can be used against an infringement suit.

37. Is there some relatively easy shortcut to obtaining permissions for copying?

Obtaining individual permissions for all photocopying of books and journals in a business setting is usually not practical, but obtaining an annual license from Copyright Clearance Center, Inc. ("CCC") provides entitlement to make unlimited copies from nearly two *million* publications on its list, but with restrictions. A CCC license permits photocopying or other hard-copy reproduction, but only for use within the organization that buys the license. For *any* use that is not internal to that organization, individual permissions must be obtained from the copyright owners in each instance. As of this writing (though this may change), a CCC license does not allow electronic sharing via a computer network or intranet, even if that use is entirely internal. The cost of a CCC license is based on the number of people (by category) in the organization, and the nature of the organization (and thus the probable nature of its photocopying of published materials). The CCC can be contacted at 222 Rosewood Drive, Danvers, Massachusetts 01923, telephone 508-750-8400, fax 508-750-4744, and URL on the World Wide Web http://www.copyright.com.

38. Is there any other way of avoiding the permission requirement of the copyright law?

In certain instances, a person may make an arrangement of a musical composition, record it, and sell the recording, even in the absence of permission from the owner of the copyright in the music. Where a phonorecord of a nondramatic musical work has been distributed to the public under the authority of the copyright owner, anyone else may make a new arrangement and recording of the work for distribution to the public as a phonorecord, provided that the basic melody or fundamental character of the work is not changed. The catch is that this right (called a compulsory license) carries with it the obligation to pay to the copyright owner a royalty for each phonorecord sold, of 2.75 cents per phonorecord or half a cent per minute of playing time, whichever yields the larger royalty payment. As a practical matter, a negotiated license often will be feasible and less expensive.

39. How is a copyright assigned or otherwise transferred?

An assignment of all interest in the copyright of a work or a transfer of any of the exclusive rights in the copyright bundle must be in writing, signed by the one transferring away the right, and all other transfers should be in writing. The only exception occurs when the rights are transferred by operation of law, under the terms of a will, or by intestate succession when the original copyright owner dies without a will. In any transfer of rights there should be no doubt about exactly what is being transferred—both in terms of the identity of the work and regarding the specific rights being transferred or assigned. There has been much expensive litigation over the years because of the lack of precision in transfer agreements, particularly concerning subsidiary rights, rights for creating derivative works, and technologies that were uncommon or unknown at the time of transfer. Drafting and negotiating agreements involving copyright transfers is not a task that should be undertaken without expert advice, or done in the context of an unbalanced negotiation in which only one side is represented by legal counsel.

40. Are there pitfalls in copyright assignments and transfers?

An assignment of a copyright means that the author no longer has *any* rights in the work, even though he or she may have spent many years producing the work and considers that it is "his" or "hers." In the absence of a contractual obligation to the contrary (and except for special rights for visual artists), the author will not even have the right of attribution once the copyright is assigned, and the assignee will be free to change the work in any way. An author should think long and hard before assigning the entire copyright. It may be sufficient to transfer limited or nonexclusive rights, or to make a total assignment while simultaneously licensing back to the author any specific, limited rights that he or she may need to have. This is especially important if the author later may wish to produce a derivative work, such as an article excerpting the work, a different version of the work, or a new work based on the old one.

41. Does the copyright owner ever have a chance to get back any of the rights that have been licensed or transferred away?

For works created prior to 1978, there are some curious and potentially beneficial situations for the copyright owner or certain relatives of a copyright owner who has died. The 1909 copyright law provided for an initial 28-year term and the opportunity for a renewal term of another 28 years. The 1976 law provided for an automatic 19-year extension of each properly registered renewal term, yielding a total copyright term of

75 years, and the 1998 amendment extended that term to 95 years. Where the original author transferred the renewal term copyright to someone else, that copyright for the "extra" 19-year term granted by the 1976 law was allowed to be recovered during a five-year window of opportunity beginning 56 years from the date the work was first published (provided, of course, that the renewal was properly registered). The 1998 amendment expands this recovery by allowing termination of a license or transfer of rights even if the window of opportunity had closed earlier. As of the effective date of the amendment, the five-year window of opportunity begins 75 years after the work's first publication (assuming proper renewal had been effected 28 years thereafter). Because of the complexities of this recapture provision, if you think this affects you, you should consider seeking appropriate counsel to assist you.

42. Can anyone else benefit from rights the copyright owner transferred away?

Another opportunity exists for the spouse, child, or grandchild of a dead author of a pre-1978 work (or for an executor, if all those relatives are dead). Regardless of what transfers of the original copyright the author may have made, those relatives have the right to the renewal term of the original copyright, but of course they must file the renewal application during the 28th year after the work's original publication. This right can be of significant value when, for example, a derivative work was created from the original work and generated interest in the original work, since the relatives' recapture of the renewal term takes away from the owner of the derivative work the right to the underlying original work. Consider, for example, an author who first published a book in 1972 and sold the entire copyright for the initial and renewal terms to a movie company that produced a derivative work (a film for television), which now has the potential for significant profits from the sales of a modified videocassette version. The widower of the author has the right to the 67-year renewal term (the original 28-year term plus the extra 19 years granted by the 1976 law plus the extra 20 years granted by the 1998 amendment) if he files the renewal application during the year 2000. Although the movie company is permitted to continue to broadcast the film for television as a valid derivative work created prior to the renewal term recapture, it may not create a new derivative work (the modified videocassette version) after the widower has recaptured the copyright renewal term, unless it negotiates a new rights transfer.

43. Is there any comparable right for post-1977 works?

The author or the surviving spouse, children, or grandchildren of a dead author (or the author's executor if all those relatives are dead) may terminate a grant of post-1977 copyright rights during a five-year window of opportunity beginning 35 years after the original grant was made. The grant may have been an assignment of the entire exclusive bundle of copyright rights, or a transfer of a portion of those rights, by exclusive or nonexclusive license. Once the grant is terminated under this provision of the copyright law, the granted rights revert and may be regranted (to the same or a different grantee) on more favorable terms. This right of termination was enacted by the Congress because of a perceived need for a provision "safeguarding authors against unremunerative transfers. A provision of this sort is needed because of the unequal bargaining position of authors, resulting in part from the impossibility of determining a work's value until it has been exploited."

44. How is this termination right exercised?

To be effective, this termination right must be exercised in a timely manner and with proper formalities. Briefly, notice of intent to terminate must be served on the one to whom the grant was originally made. The notice must specify a termination date within the five-year termination window, and must be served on the grantee not less than two years and not more than ten years before the specified termination date. The notice must be written, must be signed by one of the persons holding the termination right, and must be recorded at the Copyright Office prior to the termination date. The termination right is an inalienable one, meaning that it cannot be negotiated away, and any contract provision purporting to transfer or waive the termination right is void and unenforceable.

45. What is the effect of a transfer of a copyrighted object?

Quite simply, the transfer is *only* of the object. It does not constitute a transfer of any copyright interest in the copyrightable work embodied in the object. The purchase of a *book* brings with it the right to possess and read the book; the right to sell, rent, lend, or give it away; the right to cut it into pieces and sell the pieces, or to destroy the book entirely. What does not come with the possession of the physical book is the right to copy the book or any part of it, nor the right to read aloud from the book in public, nor the right to make a recording of a recitation from the book, nor to translate the book or any part of it except for personal use, nor to create any new work based on the book. All of those rights are part of the copyright bundle, and they are retained by the copyright owner unless and until specifically transferred.

46. Is there any difference if the transferred object is a CD or an audiocassette?

If the object being transferred is a sound recording of a song or any other musical composition, the rights that attach to the physical recording are further restricted to bar the purchaser from performing (playing) the recording publicly (to a substantial number of persons beyond a normal circle of family and friends). As mentioned earlier, there is an exception to this rule for certain music subscription services.

47. If a work of art is transferred, what happens then?

If the transferred object is a work of visual art, the original artist has special rights of "attribution and integrity" even if he or she has transferred the copyright with the object or to a third party. The Visual Artists Rights Act of 1990 expanded the control of artists over their works to an equivalent of the "moral rights" recognized by most civil-law countries (such as France) and in the Berne Convention.

48. What kinds of art are covered, and what special rights do their creators have?

A "work of visual art" is a unique painting, a unique sculpture, or a unique photograph produced solely for exhibition, as well as reproductions of these items in a signed or numbered series of no more than 200 examples. The creator of any of these objects—a visual artist—has the right to claim authorship of it, and to force attribution to be removed if the work is distorted or mutilated. Also, the visual artist can obtain the intervention of a court to enjoin an "intentional distortion, mutilation, or other modification of that work which would be prejudicial to his or her honor or reputation." Additionally, the artist can prevent the intentional or grossly negligent "destruction of a work of recognized stature." Finally, the artist may prevent an alteration to a building if that would require destruction of the artist's work of art that is integral to the building.

49.   Does the artist retain these rights under all circumstances?

There is a very large exception, which may be welcomed by artists in some circumstances. The developer of a building might decline to commission an artist to embellish the new structure for fear that the artist, through the use of the special visual art rights, would then be able effectively to block the developer from exercising full control over the building. The embellishment could be created and the artist could be paid for it, however, if the developer hired the artist as a salaried employee for the period needed to create the embellishment. The developer would then be deemed to have been the creator of the work of visual art, under the work-made-for-hire doctrine. The artist would not retain any rights in the visual art, but without the work-made-for-hire exception, there might not have been any art in the first place.

50.   Is pornography with pretensions to being art treated differently?

Unlike the federal trademark law, which bars registration of a trademark consisting of immoral, deceptive, or scandalous matter, the copyright law is deliberately neutral on the subject and treats such material no differently than any other. The creator of a blatantly indecent painting, story, or movie has exactly the same rights as would exist if the material were suitable for a church picnic of kindergarten children. If it were otherwise, the universal application of the copyright law throughout the country—an essential goal of the 1976 law—would not exist, because differing standards would be applied, depending on different people's opinions as to what is indecent. When it comes to *enforcing* the copyright law against a sexually explicit infringement, however, things are not quite so clear, and the courts have gone both ways. Claims of fair use were rejected, on both copyright and trademark grounds, for a doctored poster that showed topless cheerleaders for the Dallas Cowboys and also for an underground comic book that featured Walt Disney characters as drug-taking libertines. Nonetheless, two years later, another court declined to brand a picture showing the Pillsbury Doughboy engaging in sexual acts as a copyright infringement. The court in that case said that it did not condone the way the defendant had chosen to "assault the corporate citadel," but added that "value judgments have no place in this analysis."

51.   Do actors and musicians have any rights akin to the special rights enjoyed by visual artists?

Actors, musicians, dancers, and others who perform literary or artistic works are performers who have been given special "moral rights" under one of the 1996 treaties of the World Intellectual Property Organization ("WIPO"). In addition to the economic rights of performers, and even after the transfer of those rights, the performer has WIPO rights of "attribution and integrity" for live sound performances and for performances on phonorecords, not unlike the rights of visual artists. The right of attribution for the performance has exceptions, but the performer has the right under the WIPO treaty to object to "any distortion, mutilation, or other modification of the performance that would be prejudicial to the performer's reputation." As these "moral rights" of performers are complex and in flux, professional counsel should be sought if you believe you may be affected by them.

52.   What special rights do architects have under the copyright law?

The technical construction drawings that architects produce as necessary instructions to the builder are protected, as graphic works, from unauthorized copying, and the written specifications that generally accompany such drawings are protected in the same way as any original textual material. In addition, the actual manifestations of an architect's creativity are also protected under an amendment to the copyright law called the Architectural Works Copyright Protection Act of 1990. The *design* of the building itself (called an "architectural work" in the statute), apart from individual standard features such as doors and windows, is protected from copying, regardless of the means used. Thus, the overall form of a building as well as the arrangement and composition of the spaces and elements of the design—both interior and exterior—may not be copied by another person for a different building. For purposes of copyright law, a building is a habitable structure such as a house or an office building, as well as a structure used by people, such as a church, a warehouse, or a garage, but not one that people do not normally enter (such as a bridge or a transmission tower). The copyright in the design of a building—to the extent that its design is *original*— can be registered by filing drawings embodying that design as pictorial or graphic works. Later, after the building has been completed, photographs of the finished work can be added to the copyright record to augment the earlier drawings and describe the architect's protected design more fully. Under some circumstances a building also can be registered as a trademark.

53. How can the creator of an architectural work guard that creation?

Although the architect may seek to enjoin construction of another building whose design is substantially similar to the architect's own registered design, and may sue for damages in the event of infringement, he or she may not bar anyone from photographing or otherwise depicting the finished building that embodies that copyrighted design, and then distributing or displaying those pictorial representations of the building, if the building is located where it ordinarily is visible from a public place. Such depictions of copyrighted building designs are not prohibited by the copyright law, but in some instances pictorial representations of a building may be barred as a trademark infringement. For example, the owners of the Chrysler Building in New York City can block a photographer from selling images of its building, which is a registered trademark. The architect of a building cannot prevent the building's owner from altering the structure or destroying it. In this respect, the rights of the architect in the fruits of his or her creativity are quite different from the rights under the Visual Artists Rights Act, which enables an artist to protect the integrity of his or her reputation and work. (It is important to note that the person claiming copyright ownership in an architectural work need not be registered as an architect under applicable state law. The copyright law and the registration statutes that apply to the profession of architecture are entirely separate, and their requirements and goals are entirely different, so there is no conflict in this apparent anomaly.)

54. Are there ways in which the design of a building and the designer's rights under the copyright law are treated differently than other protected categories?

The creator of an architectural work has a copyright in the design of that work under one section of the copyright law, and a separate copyright in the related descriptive drawings under a different section of the law. Those copyrightable drawings must be deposited with the Copyright Office as part of the registration process for the copyright in them. To register the copyright in the design as embodied in the building itself, the creator may use copies of those same drawings to describe that design, or the choice may be made to use photographs of the building instead. But since there are two separate copyrights involved, there must be two separate applications, and since each application requires a deposit, the architect may find it necessary to make a double submission of the architectural construction drawings. In the event of an infringement, there may be two different causes of action, one for infringement of the building's design, and the other for infringement of the drawings describing that design, but there will be only a single recovery of damages. In addition to pursuit of damages, recourse against an infringer of a copyrighted work can extend to an injunction against continuation of the infringement, and destruction of the infringing work. Because of the potential for causing substantial harm to the infringer, and to society as well, by the possible waste of resources and economic loss generated by the destruction of an infringing building, or even by halting the construction of one that has been substantially started, an injunction in such a case is reserved solely for a plaintiff who has acted promptly. Thus, a copyright owner of an architectural work who delays in bringing an otherwise rightful infringement suit may lose the right to obtain a cessation of the infringement.

55. What does "public domain" mean?

A work in the public domain is one for which no person or group of persons or entities owns any exclusive rights. A public domain work can be freely published, copied, adapted, or otherwise used by anyone. Public domain material may stand by itself, such as the Bible, a set of tax instructions prepared by the IRS, a work that was published more than ninety-five years ago, or one for which the copyright was lost and cannot be restored (see next question). Public domain material may also lurk within an otherwise protected work. A facsimile illustration of a Form 1040 within a tax treatise for accountants, a quotation from William Shakespeare, objective facts, and an idea or concept all remain in the public domain, even when included in a work under copyright protection.

56. Are there any exceptions to the rights of the public in public domain works?

The General Agreement on Tariffs and Trade (GATT) ratified by the United States in 1994, contains a section spelling out a sub-agreement called the Trade Related Aspects of Intellectual Property Rights (TRIPS). That acronym is appropriate, as one can inadvertently trip over the *restored* private rights of a formerly public domain work. The portion of the copyright law that has been revised to accommodate GATT TRIPS will restore to its original owner the copyright lost to the public domain *if* all of the following four requirements are met.

a. At the time the work was created, at least one of the authors of the work must have been a national or domiciliary of an "eligible country," which is one, other than the United States, that is a member of the Berne Convention, the World Trade Organization, the UCC, WIPO, or the Geneva Phonograms Convention, or to which a presidential proclamation extends United States copyright protection based upon reciprocity.

b. The reason why the work is in the public domain in the country where it was first published is not that the term of copyright protection has expired.

c. The work is in the public domain in the United States because of i) lack of compliance with the formalities of United States copyright law, or ii) lack of national eligibility in the United States (for example, if the country in which it was first published then had no copyright relations with the United States), or iii) the work lacked subject-matter protection in the United States (for example, sound recordings fixed prior to February 15, 1972).

d. If published, the work must have been first published in an "eligible country" and must *not* have been published in the United States during the 30-day period following such first publication.

Despite the rather limited protection of a mandated one-year notice of the intent by the original copyright owner (or that owner's successor) to recapture the lost copyright, this can pose problems for someone who had earlier republished the then-public-domain work and still has a large warehouse inventory of the books. Negotiating an agreement with the owner of the restored copyright would be a necessity. A similar problem would exist for someone who created a derivative work from the earlier work, though there is provision in the law for continued use of the derivative work via a court-ordered mandatory license coupled with "reasonable compensation" to the copyright owner in the event that a mutually agreed-upon license agreement cannot be reached. For any TRIPS copyright restoration matter, good legal counsel and skilled negotiation clearly are essential.

57. What is a compilation?

A compilation is an assemblage of preexisting material in which the original material is not changed, but is merely selected, organized, and arranged into a new work that, as a whole, constitutes an original work of authorship. Material in the public domain, such as a collection of factual data, can be assembled into a compilation that is in itself subject to copyright. A directory is often a compilation of facts, such as a directory of attorneys (including addresses, voice and fax telephone numbers, and Internet domains) which is arranged geographically, by specialty, and by size of firm. Such a directory may be entitled to copyright protection, even though the data it contains is not.

58. What is a collective work?

A collective work is a form of compilation in which the preexisting material is subject to copyright protection separate and apart from the collective work of which it forms a part. A collective work, such as an anthology, a handbook, or a treatise, may contain some chapters for which the copyrights are owned by diverse persons, other chapters written originally by the editor who assembled the collective work, and still others that are in the public domain. The editor must analyze each component piece that goes into the work, obtain transfers of appropriate rights for those components subject to copyright, and then register the copyright in the finished collective work. Its creator is the editor if that person has done it all independently, or the work may have been produced as a work made for hire, in which case the editor's employer or the one who commissioned the work owns the copyright in the volume.

59. What is a derivative work?

A work that *derives* at least a portion of its existence from another work that is subject to copyright protection is a derivative work if the other work maintains a recognizable identity within the derivative work. A derivative work is subject to the restriction that use of the preexisting work must be with the permission of the copyright owner. The ultimate restriction comes when permission is not gained for the use of the preexisting copyrighted work. The derivative work is itself subject to copyright protection to the extent of the new material in it, but that protection is of little use where the underlying work within it has been included without a grant of appropriate rights. It would be a little like trying to sell a glass of beer without the glass. A derivative work is so tied to the original work that there *must* be agreement with the holder of the rights in the underlying material.

60.   What sorts of derivative works can there be?

As a category, derivative works are limited only by the imagination of the people involved. Think of the various Mickey Mouse and Donald Duck items that abound. They are all derivative works growing out of the original copyrighted designs of Walt Disney, and most of these derivative works were created by others under licenses from Disney. A dramatization of a book is a derivative work based on the book. The screenplay would be the first derivative work, the movie a double derivative (the book to the play to the film), and the trailer advertising the film a derivative in the third degree. Such a dramatization may (and often does) create a new work that is very far removed from the original and that appeals to a completely different audience. The income generated from the derivative work may far surpass that of the original work, but unless an appropriate agreement to transfer the necessary rights is negotiated, all that income could be lost to a lawsuit for copyright infringement. A translation to another language is a derivative work. The translation category includes a translation from the printed version in English, which can be read by humans, to an electronic version in digital code, which can be read only by a computer. An edited or revised edition of a work is a derivative work, as is a fictionalization of a biography.

61.   What effect does the derivative work have on the original?

Economically, the derivative work may effectively make the original worthless, such as a new edition of a textbook with significant updating, which destroys the market for the original. Nonetheless, the original still retains its copyright protection, and anyone wanting to borrow material from it or to create a different sort of derivative work would still need to obtain an appropriate transfer of rights. A derivative work based on a work in the public domain does not revive the original copyright (if there was one). The public domain work remains free to be used by anyone else, while the new copyrightable portions of the derivative work are subject to protection just as any original work of expression fixed in a tangible medium gains a copyright upon creation.

62. Does this mean a derivative work should be registered?

Not only should it be registered, but it should also have a proper copyright notice placed on it and it should be treated—to the extent of the material added to the underlying original—as an original copyrighted work. The same principle applies to a compilation or a collective work. To the extent of the original contribution by its creator, each of these forms of intellectual property may have value and should be just as carefully protected (with a copyright notice and registration) as a completely original work.

63. What is the significance of the words "exclusive" and "nonexclusive" in a transfer of any of the rights in the copyright bundle?

Any right transferred as an exclusive right may not be again transferred except by the one to whom it was transferred, and the original creator of the work can no longer exercise that right without the permission of the transferee. If transfers of rights are not done with care, this fact can have the unanticipated effect of curbing or restricting the original creator's other rights. A transfer of exclusive publication rights in a specific part of the world would bar publication of a derivative work in that part of the world unless the transfer were carefully phrased to restrict the exclusive publication rights to the entire work as originally written. Then the question might arise whether those exclusive rights applied only to the version printed and bound as a conventional book, or whether the intention was to include the right to make the work available electronically as part of a subscription service on the Internet. Clearly, a transfer of any exclusive right should be done very carefully, and with the aid of legal counsel. No such problem exists where the transfer is for a nonexclusive right, which can be granted to any number of persons, while still being retained by the original creator. A nonexclusive grant of permission to create one sort of derivative work does not bar a later grant for the same or a different sort of derivative work. The exclusive transfer of any of the rights in the bundle of copyright rights is tantamount to an assignment of those rights, and must be in writing, signed by the owner of the right being transferred. Recording of any exclusive rights transfer with the Copyright Office is a prudent precaution against possible infringement of the transferred rights or conflicting ownership claims.

64. What is the exclusive performance right the copyright owner holds?

The copyright owner has the right "to perform the copyrighted work publicly," which is, of course, of critical importance to the owner of the rights to a play, a movie, or a musical composition, but it also gives a poet the exclusive rights to recitations of her poetry, and to a novelist, the exclusive rights to a public reading of a work in its entirety. (As a practical matter, such public readings rarely occur, except with the works of James Joyce.) Lest you might think that reading a bedtime story to your child is a copyright violation, however, you should know that performing a work publicly means doing it in a place open to the public, or at any place where a "substantial number of persons outside of a normal circle of a family and its social acquaintances is gathered." Playing a recording of a song over the radio is a public performance that is a copyright violation of the rights of both the lyricist and the composer, unless permission has been granted or a royalty has been paid through ASCAP, BMI, or otherwise. However, this would not infringe any rights of the company that made the record of the song, nor would the musicians who recorded the song have any claim against the radio station.

65. What do ASCAP and BMI have to do with this?

The American Society of Composers, Authors and Publishers (ASCAP), Broadcast Music, Inc. (BMI), and the Society of European Stage Authors and Composers, now called SESAC, Inc., are organizations that sublicense performance rights which they have licensed from those creators of copyrighted works who are their members. These performance-rights organizations collect the royalties and remit them periodically to the rights holders, and bring infringement suits in the names of the rights holders when necessary.

66.   What is the exclusive display right the copyright owner holds?

For most copyrighted works except sound recordings (which by their nature cannot be "displayed") and any computer programs that operate invisibly within the computer circuitry, the copyright owner has the exclusive right to "display the work publicly" (the definition of "publicly" is the same as it is for a public performance). To "display" includes showing individual images from a motion picture or other audiovisual work; showing individual images together in sequence constitutes a "performance" of the movie. Of course, to "display" also means the more obvious display of a painting hanging on a wall or a piece of sculpture resting on a base, and includes showing a copy of the work, either directly or by means of a film, a slide, a televised image, or any other device or method. This means that a set designer may not hang a poster of a copyrighted painting on the wall of the stage set for a televised play without first obtaining appropriate permission, and a corporation may not scan a copyrighted magazine article into its internal database and hyperlink the article to its home page on the Internet, because sending the words out to the computer screens of the users' PCs constitutes a violation of the display right of the owner of the copyright in the article. Notwithstanding all this, there is an exception for displaying a specific copy of a copyrighted work (if lawfully made) to people gathered together where that copy physically exists. The display can be direct, or via a display device that projects a single image at a time (such as an overhead or slide projector). This permits a person to give an illustrated lecture to a live audience, which would otherwise entail special permission.

67.   How will registration of a copyright expand its protection?

Registration offers an expansion of the protections offered to an unregistered work, as follows: A copyright must be registered before an infringement suit can be filed in the United States for a claim arising after March 1, 1989, involving a work that originated in the United States. If the registration is accomplished within five years of a work's first publication, a legal presumption of the validity of the copyright and the facts on the copyright certificate is created. Recording a copyright assignment or license can give constructive notice to the world of the assignment or license, but only if the copyright is registered. Prompt registration opens up the possibility of recovering statutory damages and attorneys' fees in a successful suit against an infringer.

68. What constitutes prompt registration for purposes of statutory damages?

Statutory damages and attorneys' fees may not be awarded unless the work was registered before the infringement took place. However, there is a grace period of three months following publication, such that a registration made during that period will be deemed to have preceded any infringement that takes place during that same period.

69. When should copyright registration be done?

Generally speaking, a newly created copyrightable work should be registered as soon as it has been created, thereby gaining maximum protection for it. The effective date of copyright registration is the date on which the Copyright Office receives, in proper form, the single complete package of all material required for submission, including the filing fee. The date of receipt governs, even if it takes several months for the Copyright Office to complete the process and send the certificate of registration. If a freshly finished manuscript is to be sent out for consideration by potential agents, investors, or publishers, registration is advisable before it goes out. At the very least, a proper copyright notice should be included on the work. The date included as part of such a notice is the year the work was created, as there is not yet any publication date. If a newly developed piece of jazz music that has been perfected and rehearsed but not reduced to musical notation is to be performed before an audience, it would be good if the last rehearsal were taped and the tape registered. A new painting ought to be photographed and then registered before being hung for a public gallery showing. None of these works has been published, but for maximum protection all should be registered promptly. Later, the work as published can be registered, though this is not a requirement (as it was under the 1909 law), unless the work has been materially changed. If, as published, the work has gained three chapters and is now illustrated, for example, reregistration will ensure that the new material is as protected as the old. The copyright notice in the published work should replace the year of the work's creation with the year of its publication.

70. How does one register a copyright?

Send the appropriate completed form, the required deposit material, and the application fee, all together in one package, via certified
mail, return receipt requested, to Register of Copyrights, Copyright
Office, Library of Congress, Washington, DC 20559. Forms, instructions, and the current fee schedule are obtainable by telephoning the
Copyright Office at 202-707-3000, on the World Wide Web at
http://lcweb.loc.gov/copyright, or via Gopher at marvel.loc.gov.

71. What form should be used?

Form TX [text] is for any published or unpublished written work
that is not intended to be performed before an audience (a nondramatic work) and that is not an entire magazine, newspaper, or other periodical. This includes fiction, nonfiction, poetry, technical writing, an
individual magazine or newspaper article, a catalogue or other such
compilation, advertising copy, a letter, a speech, a pamphlet, or any
other copyrightable work made up of words. It is also used for most
computer programs. **Form TX/CON** is the continuation sheet for information that won't fit within the limits of Form TX. **Form ___/CON** is
the continuation sheet to use with all other application forms.

Form PA [performance art] is for any published or unpublished
work intended to be performed for an audience, whether directly or
indirectly. This includes a play, a screenplay, a teleplay, a radio play,
song lyrics, a musical composition, and a multimedia work.

Form VA [visual art] is for all pictorial, graphic, or sculptural
works, including pictures, photographs, maps, charts, technical drawings, pictorial labels and advertisements, and any two-dimensional or
three-dimensional art, whether fine art, commercial art, or any sort of
graphic art.

Form SR [sound recording] is for a phonograph record, a CD, a
tape, or any other device used to "fix" the sound of music or words.

Form SE Series [serial] is for any periodical, having each issue
numbered or dated in some logical fashion, that is published in successive parts with the intention to continue publishing successive issues
indefinitely. This includes a magazine, a newspaper, a newsletter or bulletin, or the regular minutes or transactions of a society. The SE Series
consists of four forms. **Form G/DN** is for one calendar month's issues
of a daily newspaper. **Form SE/Group** is for a group of issues of a

periodical that is produced as a work made for hire and published at a frequency between once a week and four times a year. **Short Form SE** is for a group of issues of a periodical whose frequency of publication is more often than once a week or less often than four times a year. **Form SE** is for registration of all other periodicals.

72. Is there some way to correct or amend a registration?

Use **Form CA** to correct an error in a copyright registration or to amplify the information given in a registration. The information provided by the registrant on this form *augments* but does not supersede what was on the earlier registration, and it does not substitute for the original registration.

73. Is there any other way to register a copyright?

An experimental program was begun early in 1996 to provide an electronic system for receipt and processing by the Copyright Office of copyright applications, deposited works, and related documents that can be transmitted securely in digital form over the Internet. This system is called CORDS, for Copyright Office Electronic Registration, Recordation and Deposit System. It is expected to reduce the processing time, from several months to only a few days or weeks, but CORDS will not be fully operative for several years, at least. The system allows an applicant to submit both the application and the actual work in digitized form via the Internet and to "sign" the submission using public key/private key encryption technology. The mandated fees are debited from the applicant's preexisting deposit account with the Copyright Office. Each digital work is assigned a unique identifier, called a "handle," through which it is accessed in the Copyright Office's secure electronic storage media. It is said that rights management information needed for licensing and permissions will be available much faster using this system. CORDS will also assist the Library of Congress (of which the Copyright Office has been a part since 1870) in expanding its digital library with new publications in addition to the older works that it is already converting to digital format.

74. Who is entitled to register a copyright?

Copyright registration can be done by anyone who owns any of the *exclusive* rights in the copyright bundle, or the authorized agent of that person. This includes a sole creator, any one of a group of joint creators, the employer of an employee who creates the work as a work made for hire, and a person who commissioned it as such. It also includes the publisher, who has the exclusive hardcover rights, the second publisher, who has the paperback rights, and the movie studio that has bought the exclusive rights to turn that blockbuster novel into a television miniseries. There is no benefit to any of these potential registrants for being the one to register the copyright. The Copyright Office does not care who registers the copyright, but will accept only one registration of a work. It must be in the name of the owner of *all* the exclusive rights in the copyright, which may be the original creator or the person to whom the creator assigned the *entire* copyright. If *fewer* than all of the exclusive rights have been transferred prior to registration, then the original holder of those rights is named as the copyright owner.

75.   How is registration handled when the work is made up of several elements, each with a different creator?

A way that is always acceptable is for the copyright in each component part to be registered separately in the name of the person who owns the rights to it. Thus, the text of a book would be in the name of its author or of the publisher to which the author had transferred *all* of his or her rights, while the illustrative photographs (permission to include them having been given) would be registered in the name of the photographer.

76.   Isn't there a simpler way that would entail only one application (and one fee)?

Registration of a group of separate works, each with a different creator, may be done as a single unit only if *all* the following conditions are met: all of the individual works are being published for the first time; they all are to be sold together as an indivisible single work; and the ownership of *all* of the exclusive rights in *each* separate work resides in the same person or organization. This means that the dust jacket of a hardcover book cannot be registered under the same application as the book itself, because it readily can be removed from the book. Similarly, illustrations for which permissions were obtained, but not complete ownership, would have to be registered separately.

77. How does this affect things like collective works, magazines, computer programs, and multimedia works?

The same principle applies. An analysis must be made of the total work to ask what elements go to make it up, who owns or originally owned the total exclusive rights to each of those elements, and whether the elements can be separated (such as the diskette, instruction manual, and binder or box for software). In each case, the owner of the work that is made up of the individual separate works can register that total work, even though such registration may not be sufficient to protect an unregistered individual component of the total work. Thus, the writer of a magazine article who has sold a one-time right of publication to the magazine publisher will not be adequately protected from infringement unless she registers her article and ensures that a copyright notice appears in a suitable place—most likely on the first page of the article as it appears in the magazine.

78. Can't a single registration suffice for a series of *unpublished* elements, such as poems, drawings, or piano sonatas, when each was created by the same person?

Here, a single registration can suffice, if what is being registered is a *collection* of poems, drawings, or any other copyrightable work. Just as the registration of a book provides protections for each individual chapter in that book, the registration of a collection of poems brings protection for each poem—not as a stand-alone work, but as part of the larger registered work. This can significantly reduce the paperwork and the fees to be paid, and can generally best be accomplished by the use of the appropriate basic form plus a continuation form (the Form ___/CON). The title of the entire collection is the name of the work on the basic form, and the detailed listing of the component elements is set forth on the continuation form. The entire collection must have been created by a single person, but if that single person is at least the cocreator of each of the works in the collection, this requirement will be deemed to have been met.

79. Can a work be registered under a pseudonym?

A book about Dutch painters of the Renaissance actually written by John Doe may be published with Johannes von Doebermann listed as the author, if the publisher believes it will help to sell the book. If Mr. Doe isn't trying to hide his true identity, the copyright registration can list the author as "John Doe, writing under the pseudonym of Johannes von Doebermann," in which case the duration of the copyright will be the same as it would be if John Doe were publishing without the pseudonym. If, on the other hand, Mr. Doe is hiding from his first wife (who is Dutch and thought she was marrying a Doebermann) and doesn't want his name connected with the book at all, the line on the copyright registration form for the author's name can be left blank, or it can say "Anonymous" or merely "Johannes von Doebermann, pseudonym." If John Doe's real name is not listed as the author, the duration of the copyright will be the same as if it had been written as a work made for hire for a corporation or other entity. However, even though the author line may be blank, there *must* be a name listed as the copyright claimant. In Mr. Doe's case, it would probably be the entity or person to whom he transferred publishing rights in the work. Later, if he finds himself in a pinch, Doe can reveal to the Copyright Office that he is in fact von Doebermann and reclaim his copyright.

80. What is the deposit material that must go along with the registration application?

For an **unpublished work**: one complete copy of the entire work.

For a **published work**: two complete copies of the best edition of the work as published as of the date of registration, except as indicated below. The best edition for this purpose is the highest quality edition in terms of printing and binding.

For a **work published only on a phonorecord**: one complete copy of the phonorecord.

For a **multimedia work**: one complete copy.

For a **motion picture**: one complete copy of the motion picture, plus a separate written description of its contents, such as a continuity, press book, or synopsis.

For a **computer program**: one visually perceptible copy of the first 25 and last 25 pages of the *source code* for the entire program. If the source code includes portions that qualify as trade secrets, there are several alternative deposits that are permissible and that will protect those trade secrets (recognizing that very few programs require that *all* source code be treated as a trade secret), as follows: a) the first 25 and last 25 pages of the entire program source code, with the trade secret portions redacted or blocked out; or b) the first 10 and last 10 pages of source code for the entire program, with no portions redacted or blocked out; or c) the first 25 and last 25 pages of *object* code for the entire program and any 10 or more consecutive pages of *source* code from the program. In cases where these requirements would require unreasonable disclosure of trade secret material, special relief may be obtained and an alternative deposit accepted.

For a **CD-ROM**: one complete copy of the CD-ROM, the operating software, and any accompanying manual, plus a copy of the identical work in print (also known as "hard copy") if it is also available in that format.

For a **three-dimensional or unique work**: identifying material such as photographs, videotapes, or drawings sufficient to describe the work visually.

For a **work first published outside the United States**: one copy of the first edition.

For **advertising materials**: one copy; for an advertisement in a magazine or other work, just the page on which it appears.

For any **separately published speech, lecture, test, or set of test answers**: one copy.

For **Form SE**: two copies of the periodical issue.

For **Short Form SE**: one copy of the individual periodical.

For **Form SE/Group**: one copy of each issue.

For **Form G/DN**: one calendar month of daily newspaper issues on positive 35mm silver halide microfilm.

For an **oversize work or a work not described here**: obtain instructions first from the Copyright Office by describing the work in a letter or telephone call.

81.   What happens to the deposit material?

It will be examined, as part of the application process, prior to acceptance of the copyright registration. It may then be taken by the Library of Congress for its permanent collections. If not, it is subject to destruction after five years, or for a fee (currently $220) the Copyright Office will retain the deposit (one copy) for the entire term of the copyright. In the event of a later infringement suit, the deposit would then be evidence of exactly what work the copyright registration covered.

82.   If a work is not registered, does that obviate the need for a deposit?

Surprisingly, the answer is "No." Even if you choose not to register a work, there is a requirement that the "owner of copyright or of the exclusive right of publication" of *each* work published in the United States make the deposit of that work within three months of publication. The validity of a copyright is *not* conditional upon this deposit being made. However, if for any reason (and at any time after publication) the Register of Copyrights discovers that the mandated deposit of your work has not been made, tracks you down, and sends a written demand for the deposit material, the penalty for not complying is a fine of $250 plus the retail price of the copies. If the refusal to comply is willful or repeated, an added fine of $2,500 may be incurred. The entire point of this requirement is, of course, to provide material for the Library of Congress at no cost to the Library.

83.   Can two people claim copyright in the same work?

Copyright can be held jointly by two creators, or by more if they have all contributed indivisible parts of the whole work. Joint authorship is quite common, and the registration forms make provision for it. It is not enough, however, for two people to decide to register a work as joint authors. The key to joint authorship is the intention, at the time each person makes a separate contribution to the work, that the separate contributions are to be merged into a unitary whole. It is the joint *creation* of that whole work that makes the joint authorship, not the joint registration. Apart from joint creation, there can also be joint ownership created by a copyright assignment, where the joint owners did not create the copyrighted work. Joint owners are treated as tenants in common, with each having the right to license and use the work, subject to the duty of accounting to the other co-owners for any profits. Each co-owner can exploit or grant nonexclusive licenses to exploit the work, but no exclusive licenses or assignment of the entire copyright can be effected without the written agreement of all the co-owners. The one exception is that any co-owner may assign his or her entire interest to a third party, who then steps into the shoes of the assigning co-owner.

84.   Is it possible for two people to claim *sole* copyright in the same work?

No . . . and yes. There can be only one person who solely created a given copyrightable work by reducing to a tangible medium a unique expression of some idea or concept. However, as ideas generally are freely flowing things, the same idea can occur to many people at the same time, and can be expressed by many people in many places. It is entirely possible that two people, each separated from the other and unaware of the other's existence, could have the same idea and could reduce it to the same form of tangible expression. While the proverbial cageful of monkeys with typewriters could not realistically be expected to produce so much as a single line of any of Shakespeare's plays, it is within the realm of reality for two people to write essentially the same simple short story without one person having copied from the other. If they were to do this, each could claim the sole copyright in the story he or she wrote, even if the stories were the same.

85. Does copyright registration make available other protection for the work?

Once a copyrightable work has been registered with the Copyright Office, that registration can be recorded with the United States Customs Service as an aid in guarding against the importation of infringing copies of the work. Cheaply made illegal foreign copies of protected CDs, tapes, books, or other works can be seized and thereby kept off the market through this process. Contact: Commissioner of Customs, IPR Branch, United States Customs Services, 1301 Constitution Avenue N.W., Washington, DC 20229.

86. How do multimedia CD-ROMs fit into the copyright scheme?

A multimedia computer product is generally marketed in the form of a CD-ROM. The term multimedia CD-ROM describes a range of products and applications that integrate multiple forms of content, such as text, images, sound, video, and graphics, with software that allows the user to access and manipulate the content on an interactive basis. A multimedia CD-ROM or other multimedia product can best be thought of in a copyright context as a compilation or collective work that may include unchanged copyrighted works, derivative works, original works, and public domain material. The multimedia product is a copyrightable work in its own right to the extent of its original material and its selection and arrangement of the preexisting works within it. Of course, the producer of the multimedia product must first obtain appropriate rights transfers or licenses from the copyright owners of the preexisting material that is included in the new work or that is used as the basis for any derivative works incorporated into the multimedia product. The producer should determine that each of those preexisting copyrightable works has been individually registered, and must also register the completed multimedia product. Because of the complexities of multimedia products, their production, marketing, and ultimate use are all tied together with a variety of licenses and contractual agreements. Intellectual property protection for their various pieces may come in the form of patent, trade secret, trademark, and contractual obligations, but copyright protections are an essential element of every multimedia product. The licenses and contracts needed for each of the component parts of the multimedia CD-ROM must be very carefully drafted to ensure that the precise rights needed by the producer of the CD-ROM are obtained. This is especially important with visual works and performances that come within the ambit of "moral rights " or their equivalent. The rights of attribution and integrity for visual artists and performers can be exercised even after the economic rights of copyright protection have been transferred or assigned by those people, thus raising the potential for problems to occur despite the contractual acquisition of copyright ownership or license. These complexities virtually dictate that anyone contemplating the production of a multimedia product include as part of the production team an attorney with the necessary specialized knowledge of copyright and other intellectual property law.

87.   What happens to the copyright law on the Internet?

Even with the passage of a major new law that addresses many areas of concern related to digital technology and the Web, there still is no clear and all-encompassing answer to that simple question. As the technology has become more advanced and more economically available, use of the Internet has expanded tremendously. Communicating via the World Wide Web is proving to be the single most effective way yet devised to enable the peoples of the world to interact peacefully for their common benefit. Part of that communication has been throwing up onto the Web a huge amount of material, thereby making it instantly available literally anywhere in the world. This sea change in information access is effecting a parallel change in how new information is developed, how it is transmitted, and how it is protected. Adding to the complexity of the Internet/copyright interplay is the ability of computers to break down a copyrighted work—writings, sounds, images—into digital fragments. Those fragments can be recombined into a perfectly reproduced clone of the original, or they can be combined with bits and pieces of other works to create derivative works or entirely new works. The possibilities are virtually infinite, and they are available to people in other countries whose copyright laws are at odds with, or ignore, the copyright law of the United States.

Two increasingly viable ways of protecting information in cyberspace are through digital encryption and through the inclusion of copyright management information with the actual copyrighted material. Digital encryption enables the sender to scramble the information electronically (akin to the old-fashioned use of coded messages in print) and permits a receiver who possesses the digital "key" to unscramble the code and read the message. Copyright law now provides certain limited protections against wrongful hacking into an encrypted transmission and wrongful "reverse engineering" of a computer program. Copyright management information means data, electronically embedded in a digitally transmitted copyrighted work or otherwise attached to it, that identify the owner of the work and that give conditions for its use or other details. Such information is necessary for effective control of Web-accessed material. Serious penalties may be imposed for tampering with that information or for "breaking and entering" an encrypted transmission.

U.S. copyright law now recognizes and encourages the development and implementation of technological protection measures that enable copyrighted material to be transmitted in digital format readily and securely for commercial or educational use. As these techniques evolve, this will make it easy to "borrow" a book or a phonorecord in digital form from a library, or to purchase one from a store. However, because of the uncertainty of these new technologies, Congress has mandated that they be monitored and that their effect be assessed annually. Additional legislation concerning copyrighted materials on the Internet is anticipated.

88. In the meantime, what happens to copyright law *right now* on the Internet, and how should a user approach material that is available on-line?

With this question, we are back to basics. Treat the Internet no differently than any other place where information is available. In effect, it is a library, with books, pictures, and records on the shelves, most of which should be assumed to be subject to conventional copyright restrictions, even when there is not a copyright notice in sight and the name of the author is not readily found. Treat Web resources with as much caution and observance of the copyright law restrictions as you would if you were dealing solely with traditional information resources. Stay honest and sleep with a clear conscience. The copyright owner of a text file, a graphic image, or a recording on the Internet possesses the same bundle of rights, described earlier in this book, as does any other copyright owner. That owner has the exclusive right to copy and distribute the work, so don't use a few keystrokes and mouse-clicks to send a work you find on the Internet to all your friends. Copying and distributing a work in the 18th century meant laboriously printing it on a hand-operated press, binding it by hand using needle and thread, and delivering the resultant books by foot or with the aid of a horse or ox. Merely because we can accomplish the same thing two centuries later in a minute or two electronically does not change the essence of what is being done. Don't let ease of exploitation obscure the essential underlying rights of others.

89. Doesn't the fact that the material was uploaded to the Internet show that it was deliberately made available for downloading and use?

The question has not been decided by a court, but it seems to be reasonable to assume that when the *copyright owner* of a work uploads that work to a bulletin board service or a Web site, an implied license is created for any surfer on the net to download that work for *personal* use, including printing out an image or text file or listening to a music file. The catch, of course, is that only the legitimate owner of the relevant rights can upload the work, and the user who encounters that work through a hyperlink has no way of determining who put it there in the first place. Just as a thief cannot give good title to property that is stolen, a cyber-thief cannot grant a license he does not rightfully possess. It has already been determined in court that a person who wrongfully *uploads* a work onto the net can be held liable for copyright infringement. However, when someone innocently *downloads* a work that should never have been uploaded in the first place, and then uses what was downloaded only for personal purposes, that someone has not done anything wrongful.

90. Does nonpersonal use after downloading become legitimate if the work is significantly changed so that it is then a new work?

If the downloaded work essentially is used only as an inspiration or jumping-off point, and is so changed as to be completely unrecognizable in the new work, then that nonpersonal use is acceptable. Anything less than that, however, may be considered a *derivative* work, for which permission to use the original work must first be obtained from the copyright owner. As with all adaptations or recastings of original creative works, the dividing line separating a derivative work from a totally new copyrightable work cannot be demarcated in a fixed and definable way. Consciously or unconsciously, *all* human creativity is based to one degree or another on earlier works; no person labors *totally* in a vacuum. The result is a hazy area, without fixed boundaries, between what is sufficiently new as to provide a basis for copyright protection for the entire work, and what is a derivative work for which copyright protection does not extend to the prior material it contains. Lack of clear answers for questions like this one is why this book includes a warning that legal counsel may be needed in specific instances to determine what is and is not allowable under applicable copyright law.

91. How do the rules apply to on-line databases and to works in the public domain that are accessed through Web site hyperlinks?

Any work in the public domain is freely available for use and adaptation by anyone, but—and this is a big but—any derivative work based on a work in the public domain is a new copyrightable work to the extent of whatever it contains that is *not* in the public domain. The Bible, found on a Web site, can be downloaded or retransmitted anywhere, but if a hyperlink at a specific verse yields an analysis of that verse, the analysis is not public domain material, even if it includes a portion of the text of the verse. However, if clicking on a given word pattern provides a comprehensive list of all other uses of that word pattern and the book:chapter:verse location of each such use, that list might be freely usable—not because its basis is the Bible, which is in the public domain, but because it is merely a list of facts. The location in any book of a specific word pattern is a fact; a fact is considered to belong to everyone and thus does not merit copyright protection. Many on-line databases are similar compilations of facts. The 1996 WIPO conference rejected a proposed treaty that would have made the *factual content* of digital databases fully copyrightable and the U.S. Congress declined to enact an amendment similar to its significant 1998 revision and expansion of the copyright law. Nonetheless, when a database permits the user to gain access to facts categorized and arranged in specific ways, the *arrangement* of the database, which may be the result of specialized knowledge and creative effort, may be protected under the copyright law as a compilation, but the underlying factual material remains unprotected. Because these few questions can only scratch the surface of the copyright issues concerning information found on the World Wide Web, a net browser should look very carefully at the "small print" accompanying any on-line information, to discover any copyright warnings or other restrictions on use—*before* downloading material. Caution and an awareness of potential copyright issues always should guide the hand that guides the mouse.

92. Should special precautions be used when uploading to the Internet copyrighted information that you are not willing to share with others for free?

Although it may be difficult to determine copyright limitations on information belonging to others that is available two mouse-clicks away on the World Wide Web, protect *your* information by making it clear to all that *you* own it. Register your work properly *first*. Then put it out on the Web if you wish, but only after ensuring that copyright notices and expanded warnings are placed strategically where the reality of anticipated usage of the work suggests that they will be most likely to be seen and heeded. Copyright infringement of material on the Web can be very difficult to detect and even more difficult to prosecute. Assume that misuse of your work will go unpunished, so aim to discourage any such misuse from the start. Also, adjust your financial dreams for your work to the reality of a very changed world. Recognize that, right now, absolute control of every use, display, performance, and copy of a copyrighted work is not achievable in cyberspace—and possibly this will remain true forever. Consider this factor when constructing financial projections for your own copyrighted work, and weigh the desirability of splitting your goals. Perhaps you can give away some of your work by making it freely available on the Web, while retaining full control of other parts of your work by keeping it off the Web. Know the structure and protections of copyright, accept the reality of the wide-open Web, and work those factors into your plans for what you create.

93. What happens if a person infringes upon someone else's copyright?

Nothing, unless someone whose legally protected interests are harmed by the infringement does something about it. When a suspected violation of one's copyright interests is encountered, a possibly aggrieved person should seek legal counsel before doing *anything*. As with any potential lawsuit, determining the general scope of the specific facts and circumstances is the critical first step, followed by a legal analysis to determine whether in fact an infringement has occurred. This is not necessarily a simple matter, since the copyright law gives only the skeleton of the copyright scheme; one must also look at the actual court decisions in lawsuits covering copyright issues. These decisions provide the rulings that flesh out and give form to what constitutes copyright law beyond the bare words of the statute. It is only by searching out final court rulings from cases similar to the matter at hand that the copyright attorney can find specific usable guidance in determining whether a copyright infringement is likely to exist under the specific fact pattern presented.

94. Is there a simple initial test for determining what is *not* an infringement?

Some allowable uses are clear-cut, such as a use under one of the statutory "compulsory licenses," or the limited public display of a work by the owner of the physical copy or phonorecord. Also clearly not an infringement is the use of the basic *idea* in the copyrighted work, apart from its *expression*. Beyond that, the specific facts and circumstances have to be measured against court-decided cases with similar or analogous facts and circumstances.

95. Assuming that a given situation is clearly an infringement, what can be done?

Because litigation is an expensive and often chancy route for obtaining redress for a legal wrong, there should be (as in nearly all disputes) an initial dialogue with the infringer to determine if some sort of alternative dispute resolution can be effected. If the infringement was "innocent," perhaps because the work didn't bear a copyright notice or was found under circumstances that suggested to the infringer that it was in the public domain, a presentation of simple proof of the copyright owner's rights may be enough to convince the infringer to stop the infringement. If the infringer has already invested significant capital, a negotiation may yield a solution that will allow the infringer to cut some of the loss while still affording the copyright owner a relatively undiminished value for the rights in the copyrightable work. Creative negotiation may permit the infringer to recoup the entire investment in the infringing use and still provide for the copyright owner some unrelated benefit that will balance the scales. Devoting a reasonable amount of time, money, and effort to an attempt to develop a workable solution to an infringement situation is often a wise investment to avoid the heavy burden of litigation.

96. If negotiation fails, how does one proceed?

For a work first published in the United States, the initial hurdle is copyright registration. Even when a copyright infringement produces a valid cause of action, a claim cannot be brought to enforce the violated rights of a domestic work unless the copyright has been registered with the Copyright Office, as outlined earlier in this book. However, as one of the changes in the copyright law needed to permit the United States to join the Berne Convention, Congress removed the registration prerequisite to a copyright infringement suit for works that were first published in other Berne Convention member countries.

97. Who can bring suit for infringement and where is the suit brought?

The plaintiff who files a copyright infringement suit must be the person or business entity that owns the specific exclusive right at issue, or the one entitled to receive royalties from the exercise of that right. Because the copyright law is a federal law, a suit involving a violation of that law is heard in a federal district court in whatever district has personal jurisdiction over the infringer. Personal jurisdiction, which applies to corporations as well as natural persons, lies in the district in which the infringer lives or has a place of business, or where there is sufficient "connection" with the infringer or the infringement to meet the standards set under federal procedural law.

98. Are there any limits on when the suit can be brought?

There is a time limit on when a suit can be brought, set by something called a statute of limitations. For a copyright infringement claim, the suit must be filed with the proper court within three years after the copyright owner actually knew or should have known that the infringement took place. If more than three years have elapsed since the infringement, and the copyright owner in fact did not have knowledge of the infringement during that three-year period, there may be a question of whether the owner *should* have known the copyrighted work was being infringed. This can be a complicated matter. If potential recoveries warrant the effort, it may be appropriate to have competent legal counsel investigate the potential for bringing suit successfully.

99.   What must be proved to win a suit for infringement?

Infringement can occur by the defendant violating any of the exclusive rights of the copyright owner, including going beyond what a valid license to use the work specifically permitted. The most common form of infringement is improper copying. Some examples of this kind of infringement are: improperly making a few hundred photocopies of a one-page work and distributing them to employees of some organization for political ends; printing, binding, and selling a pirated edition of a best-selling novel for profit; or wrongfully using parts of a copyrighted work within a new work to further an academic career. There are three basic elements needed to prove infringement by copying: a) ownership of a work protected by a valid copyright; b) copying of the work by the infringer; and c) improper use of the work's protected expression by the infringer.

100.   If the work is copyrighted, why must that be proved?

The first of the three elements actually has three subelements. There must be a *valid* copyright protecting the *specific* work (or portion of the work), and the plaintiff must *own* the specific exclusive right that was allegedly infringed upon. The registration, which is the first prerequisite to enable a copyright infringement suit of a work first published in the United States, does not in itself prove that the copyright is valid. However, if the work was registered within five years of its first publication, it is presumed to be protected by a valid copyright and whoever is listed as the copyright owner on the registration is presumed to be the true owner. This considerable benefit of prompt registration means that you, as plaintiff, do not need to prove that your work is original (often a difficult thing to prove, as it entails proving a negative—that the work was not copied from anything else), and that you do not need to prove that it was you who actually created it (or that you properly received the ownership by assignment from the original owner). Because this timely registration creates only a presumption, however, the defendant has the right to prove the opposite, thereby disproving your claim.

101.   How is copying proved without having videotaped or recorded something that happened when no one other than the infringer knew anything wrong was going on?

As an alternative to proving *actual* copying, it is acceptable to prove that the infringer had *access* to the work and that the infringer's work or the relevant part of that work is *substantially similar* to the original work. Access is presumed if your work is published and generally available to the public, and it is not necessary to prove that the infringer actually bought or possessed a copy. Access to an unpublished work must be proved much more specifically, even though circumstantial evidence may suffice. *Substantial similarity* or the lack thereof has been the subject of numerous lawsuits. Two of the most well-known cases involved the Alfred Hitchcock thriller *Rear Window* and the play *Abie's Irish Rose*. It is not necessary to prove word-for-word copying, but there must be substantial similarity that is evident to the ordinary viewer or reader, and the various possible alternative reasons for such similarity must have been eliminated as causes, so that the conclusion that copying *must* have occurred becomes inescapable. It is usually those alternative reasons that derail a legal finding of substantial similarity. Among such possible explanations for apparent similarity could be that: both works are based on the same historical events and research materials; or both works use the same public domain material and commonplace expression; or both works fit into a genre of popular style and plot that permits little variation; or both works were plagiarized from the same sources; or the similarities are simply coincidental.

102.   What does "improper use of the work's protected expression" mean?

The *protected expression* is the independently created sequences of words and the selection and arrangement of the material in the work. No public domain material in the work, and none of the work's facts and ideas, are within the scope of the copyright protection. At the most obvious, a pirated work would encompass the copying verbatim of all of the protected expression. Where only part of the work is copied, it must be shown that what was copied was not the public domain, factual, or purely conceptual aspects of the work. More difficult to show is improper copying where the protected expression has been paraphrased. At some point a paraphrase veers so far from the original as to be a new work, not unlike the fuzzy area between a derivative work and a new creation. Exceedingly difficult to demonstrate, and thus to prove, is copying of a work's total original concept and ambience. That might seem to be easy to accomplish, if the work in question were a harpsichord sonata by Domenico Scarlatti or a Luck and Pluck story by Horatio Alger, but skilled musicians and writers have shown that it is possible convincingly to imitate either of these categories of creative works without infringing upon their nonexistent copyrights, because both creators used commonplace themes, repetitive structures used by many creators, and standard note patterns or stock characters, all of which would be unprotected elements under our copyright law.

103. Is there any time when clear copying of protected expression is not improper?

Even if the protected expression of the original is used in the allegedly infringing work, it may be excused if it falls under the *fair use* exception, as might happen in a scholarly or educational work, or when the work is used for other nonprofit purposes. Sometimes a writer has no choice but to copy or paraphrase the words of another. If the original expression is one of very few ways reasonably possible to express a specific idea or fact, the expression is considered as having merged with the underlying idea or fact, thereby allowing it to be *properly* copied. This is called the "merger doctrine." It applies primarily to nonfiction works for which the underlying facts are so specific and limited that expressing them creatively is problematic.

104. Once the elements are established and the infringement is proved, what relief is available to the plaintiff?

An important remedy available in any successful infringement suit is a permanent injunction, which is a judicial order from the court telling the infringer to stop infringing, and an additional order that all infringing material be impounded and destroyed along with the negatives, plates, masters, or other paraphernalia used to create the infringing material. It is even possible to obtain a temporary injunction long before a full-fledged trial, if the plaintiff can show to the judge (and the defendant cannot sufficiently rebut that showing) that the suit is likely to be successful, and that the plaintiff will suffer significant harm if the infringer is not ordered to stop infringing in advance of the trial. To obtain such an injunction, however, the plaintiff will have to post a bond to cover the damage to the defendant from the injunction if the plaintiff in fact does not win at trial. In an exceptionally critical situation (such as the week before a magazine is going to publish an issue containing the last pages of a soon-to-be-released cliff-hanger murder mystery), a copyright owner can seek a ten-day temporary restraining order ("TRO") from a judge without the potential infringer being present. A hearing with both sides present would then be promptly scheduled for arguments on whether the TRO should be replaced upon its expiration by a temporary injunction, as described above.

105. In addition to destruction of the offending material and a permanent injunction against the infringer, can money damages be obtained?

In relation to monetary damages, a significant advantage of timely copyright registration comes into play. Timely registration of an unpublished work is registration done prior to the date of the infringement of the unpublished work. For a published work, registration is timely if it is done either within three months of the date of first publication or before the infringement began. When an infringement suit is successful and there was timely registration, the plaintiff may choose between receiving actual damages plus excess lost profits, or special statutory damages. If the registration was not timely, only actual damages that are proved to the satisfaction of the court can be recovered.

106. What comprises proven actual damages?

Proven actual damages would include all the losses shown, to the satisfaction of the court, to have been sustained by the copyright owner as a result of the infringement—all the money shown *not* to be in the copyright owner's pocket as a result of the infringing acts of the defendant. Such damages might include reduced sales of the original work, opportunities for further exploitation of the original work that were lost because of the infringement, and injury to the reputation of the copyright owner. In addition, if the proven actual damages are less than the infringer's profits from the infringing material, the plaintiff can claim those profits that are in excess of the actual damages.

107.   What are the statutory damages available to a timely registrant?

An award of statutory damages does not require that the plaintiff prove actual losses in terms of dollars, but the amount of such an award is entirely within the discretion of the judge, within certain limits. If the court finds that the infringer acted *innocently* by sincerely believing that he was not infringing, the judge may award as little as $200. Innocent infringement will not be found, however, if the defendant had access to copies of the original work that contained a valid copyright notice. (This is another reason to include such a notice as a routine matter.) If the court finds that the infringer acted *willfully*—he knew he had no right under the law to use the original work, but he nonetheless went ahead and used it—the judge may award damages up to $100,000. If, however, the court finds that the infringer acted neither innocently nor willfully, the judge may award between $500 and $20,000 for all infringements by a single infringer of a single work. If there are multiple works that were infringed, an award may be made for each such work. If there are multiple defendants, each of whom was an infringer independently of the others, an award may be made against each such defendant. There can, however, be only a single statutory award against an individual infringer of a specific work, regardless of how many plaintiffs there are and how many times the infringement happens. As a practical matter, however, unless the actions of the infringer were egregious, these awards tend to be relatively small. This factor should be considered when deciding whether to take the trouble of proving actual damages, and whether to bring the suit in the first place.

108.   Can a plaintiff also recover court costs and the fees of an attorney and her expense disbursements?

If the copyright owner made a timely registration of the copyright and succeeds in the infringement suit, the judge has the discretionary power to decide what a reasonable fee is to provide recompense for the owner's attorney and what reasonable disbursements should be, and then to order the defendant to pay that sum to the plaintiff. Affecting this calculation are questions of whether any of the parties acted in bad faith or unreasonably, and whether the plaintiff, in bringing the action, helped to advance the state of copyright law or to establish or defend important legal principles.

109.   Is there a downside to this opportunity for recovery of the attorney's fees?

There is, perhaps, a downside from one perspective, which may be seen as a leveling of the playing field from another viewpoint. If the alleged infringer successfully defends against the infringement claim, the judge may turn the tables and order the plaintiff to pay the defendant's attorney's reasonable fees and expenses. According to a 1994 decision of the Supreme Court, judges must treat both sides evenhandedly, by using the same criteria to determine awards for attorneys' fees and expenses, regardless of which side wins. This makes copyright litigation even more risky for the "little guy," and provides an additional incentive to negotiate a resolution to an infringement situation instead of bringing a lawsuit.

110.   Are there other possible penalties for a defeated infringer?

The copyright law provides for criminal penalties for a willful infringer whose motive was to seek a commercial advantage. When a misdemeanor conviction occurs, penalties can range up to $10,000 and one year in jail. If the infringement is tape piracy, the possible penalty for a first offense is $25,000 and one year in jail, and for a second offense, $50,000 and two years in jail. In addition, the court can order forfeiture, destruction, or other disposition of infringing copies and the equipment used in their manufacture. However, criminal actions in copyright cases are very rare, and generally involve large-scale commercial piracy. There also are significant penalties (up to $1 million and ten years in jail) for wrongfully defeating encryption technologies or wrongfully providing or changing digital copyright management information.

111.   Is that the extent to which criminal law and copyright law intersect?

At the lesser level of a violation, the copyright law provides that falsely representing a material fact in a copyright application or other written statement filed in connection with an application carries a fine of up to $2,500. A maximum fine in the same amount may be imposed on one who fraudulently removes or alters a copyright notice on a copyrighted work, or who fraudulently places a copyright notice on an item, or who fraudulently distributes—or imports with intent to distribute—an item with a copyright notice on it that the person knows to be false. Again, these remedies usually are sought only in especially flagrant cases.

112. Is there any other way to recover for the infringement or other improper use of a copyrighted work?

If the copyright owner has entered into a license agreement with another person who then infringes the copyright owner's rights or otherwise uses the copyrighted work improperly under the terms of the license, the owner can bring an action under applicable state contract law. If the licensee went beyond the rights granted under the license, contract damages can be sought. However, because of the preemption by the 1976 federal copyright law of all state law granting rights that are equivalent to the exclusive rights granted by the federal law and that cover the same subject matter, an aggrieved copyright owner cannot use the existence of a license agreement in an attempt to gain state court jurisdiction over an action that actually lies within the ambit of the copyright law and thus must be heard in federal court. If there is a valid contract claim under state law in addition to the federal copyright law claim, under federal procedural law the contract claim may be joined with the copyright claim if the two are so connected that pursuing them separately in separate forums might result in conflicting results. On occasion, a less important federal copyright claim may be appended to a predominantly state-law-related contract claim. This area is quite complex and difficult to sort out. In any event, if you reach the point of having to make choices in such a situation, you will have retained legal counsel already.

113. Do I now have all the answers?

If you did, this book would put a legion of copyright attorneys out of business overnight. What you should have now is more questions. We have skimmed the surface of copyright law, to alert you to areas where there may be problems and pitfalls and to suggest areas where it may be prudent to move carefully within the intellectual property thicket. Copyright law has many areas of great clarity, but there also are areas where absolute answers are rare, and guidance is gained only through a reasoned interpretation of a series of court decisions analyzed as a group. The goals of this book will have been achieved if you now understand the scope of the subject, if you have grasped the main points, and if you can recognize when your specific set of facts and circumstances calls for professional advice and guidance.

114. Why are there 113 questions above when the title of this book says 101?

A basic rule of Dover Publications is never to promise more than what a book delivers, and always to deliver more than what the reader expects.

Andrew Alpern is special counsel with the international law firm of Hughes Hubbard & Reed LLP, which maintains a vigorous practice in all aspects of intellectual property law. Mr. Alpern's other books with Dover Publications include *New York's Architectural Holdouts* (ISBN 0-486-29425-0), *Historic Manhattan Apartment Houses* (ISBN 0-486-28872-2), *Luxury Apartment Houses of Manhattan* (ISBN 0-486-27370-9), and *New York's Fabulous Luxury Apartments* (ISBN 0-486-25318-X). He also has published the *Handbook of Specialty Elements in Architecture* and *Alpern's Architectural Aphorisms,* and has completed *The New York Apartment Houses of Rosario Candela and James Carpenter: a Descriptive Catalogue.* Alpern is an architect and an architectural historian as well as a practicing attorney.